HAL•LEONARD
INSTRUMENTAL
PLAY-ALONG

AUDIO
ACCESS
INCLUDED

PLAYBACK+
peed • Pitch • Balance • Loop

TROMBONE

Disney

Encanto

T0071623

Audio arrangements by Peter Deneff

To access audio visit:
www.halleonard.com/mylibrary

Enter Code
7783-6038-9631-6644

ISBN 978-1-70516-360-3

HAL•LEONARD®

Visit Hal Leonard Online at
www.halleonard.com

Contact us:
Hal Leonard
7777 West Bluemound Road
Milwaukee, WI 53213
Email: info@halleonard.com

In Europe, contact:
Hal Leonard Europe Limited
42 Wigmore Street
Marylebone, London, W1U 2RN
Email: info@halleonardeurope.com

In Australia, contact:
Hal Leonard Australia Pty. Ltd.
4 Lentara Court
Cheltenham, Victoria, 3192 Australia
Email: info@halleonard.com.au

ALL OF YOU

TROMBONE

Music and Lyrics by
LIN-MANUEL MIRANDA

COLOMBIA, MI ENCANTO

TROMBONE

Music and Lyrics by
LIN-MANUEL MIRANDA

THE FAMILY MADRIGAL

TROMBONE

Music and Lyrics by
LIN-MANUEL MIRANDA

DOS ORUGUITAS

TROMBONE

Music and Lyrics by
LIN-MANUEL MIRANDA

SURFACE PRESSURE

TROMBONE

Music and Lyrics by
LIN-MANUEL MIRANDA

WAITING ON A MIRACLE

TROMBONE

Music and Lyrics by
LIN-MANUEL MIRANDA

rit.

WE DON'T TALK ABOUT BRUNO

TROMBONE

Music and Lyrics by
LIN-MANUEL MIRANDA

WHAT ELSE CAN I DO?

TROMBONE

Music and Lyrics by
LIN-MANUEL MIRANDA